LEADERS OF THE SCIENTIFIC REVOLUTION™

FRANCIS BACON

MARYELLEN LO BOSCO

Rosen YA™

New York

Published in 2018 by The Rosen Publishing Group, Inc.
29 East 21st Street, New York, NY 10010

First Edition

Library of Congress Cataloging-in-Publication Data

Names: Lo Bosco, Maryellen, author.
Title: Francis Bacon / Maryellen Lo Bosco.
Description: First Edition. | New York : Rosen Publishing, 2017. | Series: Leaders of the scientific revolution | Includes bibliographical references and index.
Identifiers: LCCN 2016055888 | ISBN 9781508174660 (library bound)
Subjects: LCSH: Bacon, Francis, 1561-1626.
Classification: LCC B1197 .L595 2017 | DDC 192—dc23
LC record available at https://lccn.loc.gov/2016055888

Manufactured in China

CONTENTS

INTRODUCTION

Sir Francis Bacon, embodiment of the Renaissance and a Renaissance man, was a statesman, politician, philosopher, essayist, historian, and visionary. Bacon heard the faint yet distinct clarion call of humankind's next evolutionary leap forward. He was the earliest of the empirical philosophers, believing that sense perceptions were the best portals to receive knowledge of the external world. He was one of the first philosophers of modern science and the first Western philosopher to say that science and religion should operate in separate realms so that both could remain true to their own particular purpose and calling. Bacon did not lead the Scientific Revolution; rather, he helped create the philosophical foundation upon which it could build its edifice.

Although born into a privileged family with access to the highest circles of power, Bacon was unlucky in developing his political career. He lost his father prematurely, before he could establish himself in the court of England's queen, Elizabeth I. His powerful uncle, William Cecil, Lord Burghley, was an advisor to the queen; but he was of little help, being somewhat jealous that his brilliant nephew outshone his own son, Robert Cecil. Bacon also tripped himself up, crossing

Sir Francis Bacon was made Viscount St. Albans in 1621, the same year he was disgraced by his enemies. He kept his titles but lost his seat in Parliament.

Elizabeth and aligning himself with the unfortunate Robert Devereux, the second Earl of Essex, who gradually fell from favor and was tried for treason. When James I ascended the throne, Bacon's luck changed, and he eventually became lord chancellor. But once again, he was cast down, as his enemies conspired against him.

Throughout his tumultuous political career, Bacon wrote essays, philosophical books about the purpose and practice of science, law treatises, religious meditations, and even fiction. Bacon hoped to complete an encyclopedic work, called *Instauratio Magna* (*The Great Instauration*), in which he would reorder all the fields of study and put science and "the mechanical arts" on their proper footing. He strongly objected to the way in which the philosophers of his time—primarily the Scholastics—had taken every word of Aristotle as absolute truth. In an effort to reconcile Greek philosophy with Christian dogma, the Scholastics created a philosophical system whose primary purpose came to be the construction of elegant and irrefutable logical arguments rather than the pursuit of the truth. Moreover, the methods of the Scholastics had spilled over into other areas of study, impeding the development of science, in Bacon's view. The meaning of "instauration" is "restoral" or "renewal," and Bacon made it his task to create an intellectual renewal in Western thought and build an intellectual body of work that would rival Aristotle's. Thus, he wrote the *Novum Organum* (*New Organon*) to refute Aristotle's *Organon* and *The New Atlantis* to retell Plato's story of the world's mythical golden age. Bacon believed that human beings had a right to knowledge and dreamed of reinstating man to his proper position as master of nature—an office Bacon and others believe that he had lost with his fall from Paradise. While Bacon did not complete his great work, he succeeded in making a profound impact on Western science and the dazzling future it created.

CHAPTER ONE

From the First Millennium to the Beginning of Secular Culture

To understand Francis Bacon, the man who helped build the modern framework for scientific inquiry, we first must examine the soil in which his ideas grew. The Middle Ages, beginning roughly in 476 CE with the fall of the Roman Empire, was a long, sometimes dark period in European history that preceded the Renaissance and Scientific Revolution.

Everything the typical medieval man or woman believed or experienced was based on a unified and pervasive religious vision of life. Although parts of Europe had Jewish and Muslim communities, the majority of people lived in a world governed by Christian orthodoxy, in which alternative views were nonexistent. Even kings were subject to the pope in Rome. Nonetheless, ordinary people's beliefs were an admixture of Christianity and tribal religion that predated the Christian conversion of Western Europe. Thus, orthodox Christian practice incorporated folk beliefs and tribal myths. The forces of omnipotent nature were outside of human control, although they might be influenced or appeased by prayer, magic, or ritual. The medieval mind gave way in the years leading up to the Scientific Revolution, as people began to see themselves as individuals and nature as a phenomenon outside of themselves that could be observed, understood, and even manipulated.

THE MIDDLE AGES

At the end of the fifth century, the western part of the Roman Empire was conquered by Germanic barbarians, mostly running from the Huns, who had invaded Europe from Mongolia. In the lands of former empire, a widespread conversion to Christianity—which had become the religion of the Roman Empire in the fourth century—took place among both old and new tribes. During the Middle Ages, recurring bouts of famine and plague killed off large swaths of the population. Roads (except for Roman roads) fell into disrepair, and many skilled trades disappeared. Throughout most of the Middle Ages, serfs made up between 80 and 90 percent of the European population. Serfs were peasants who were bound to the land they leased and lived under a feudal lord in a condition of servitude. It was not until the fourteenth century that serfdom started dying out and people who had been serfs became free peasants.

The Christians of Europe, converted from

so-called pagan religions, held onto many of their old beliefs. The church accommodated the converts, partly by ignoring some of the old practices and partly by incorporating them into Christian practice. Over time, however, the Roman Catholic Church became an autocratic institution, ruling the people with an iron fist. The church owned about a third of Western Europe's land by the thirteenth century and had made

MONASTERIES PRESERVE THE INTELLECTUAL CAPITAL OF THE WEST

Even though the church sought to control ideas that would challenge its authority, it also became a champion of intellectual life. The great library of Alexandria, Egypt, was destroyed in the first millennium and the ruin of the Roman Empire included decimation of schools, libraries, and other institutions of learning. The church picked up where the academies and libraries of the ancient world had left off, and the monasteries of Europe kept the flame of Western culture burning. The first Benedictine monastery was founded in 529 CE. Monasteries in Ireland began to flourish in the same time period. Additional orders of monastics were established throughout Western Europe in the centuries that followed. The monks preserved knowledge about agriculture and animal husbandry and made contributions to the technical arts, such as mining and metallurgy. Perhaps even more important, they created manuscripts. During the early Middle Ages, most of the knowledge of the Greeks had been lost. By the thirteenth century, however, translations of Aristotle (from Arabic, in which the works had been preserved by Muslim scholars) were reintroduced into Europe. Monks and nuns preserved texts by copying them, and the monasteries became centers for learning, evidenced by the fact that the nobility sent their sons to the monastery for an education.

Aristotle was enthusiastically taken up and studied in the monasteries. Though some of Aristotle's teachings contradicted those of the church, Christian scholars and philosophers, such as Thomas Aquinas, found a way to integrate them with Christian theology. This was the beginning of the movement called Scholasticism, which applied Aristotle's logic to theological questions. As time went on, Scholasticism—both a school of philosophy and an approach to learning—migrated to the universities and was applied beyond theology to other fields of study.

itself rich through corruption carried out at the highest levels. Those who significantly deviated from Catholic beliefs were usually tortured, killed, or excommunicated, meaning a person was thrown out of the Christian community forever. People quaked in fear at the threat of excommunication, which not only signaled social death, but was also thought to result in damnation—or spending eternity in hell.

THE REFORMATION AND THE RENAISSANCE

The church slowly loosened its grip on the populace, beginning in the fourteenth century, as three historical episodes broadened cultural and intellectual thought. First, new knowledge from the Muslim world that the Christians brought back from the Crusades (1095–1291) became integrated into European culture. Second, the European explorers who voyaged east to India and China and west to the Americas returned with information about people who looked different and had different languages, customs, and religious practices. Third, some Roman Catholics rebelled against church corruption that had gone unchecked for centuries, launching the Protestant Reformation.

The Protestant Reformation won over the hearts and minds of some of Europe's Christians, turning them away from the church of Rome. The Lutheran revolution (starting in 1517), led by Martin Luther in Germany, was followed by two other schisms inspired

Medieval Christians pictured hell as a realm of eternal suffering, as seen in this twelfth-century painting in which an angel closes hell's gate on the damned.

by the French theologian John Calvin (in 1530) and Henry VIII, king of England (in 1534). Both created their own sects of Christianity. Once the floodgates opened, additional Christian sects formed over the next

Pictured in this woodcut is Martin Luther, who began the Protestant Revolution when he nailed 95 theses criticizing corrupt church practices to a church door in Wittenberg, Germany, in 1517.

few centuries. While the Protestant revolution loosened Catholicism's grip on Europe, early Protestantism ended up being just as dogmatic and persecutory as the mother church it broke away from. In response to the Protestant revolution, the Catholic Church launched the Counter-Reformation (1545), which corrected some of the church's abuses but also reestablished the persecution of the Inquisition.

The Renaissance (which means "rebirth") began in Italy in 1350 and spread to England by the first decades of the 1500s. The Renaissance was a pan-European phenomenon that encompassed

- a new interest in classical Greek and Roman texts
- the early discoveries of the Scientific Revolu-

tion

- a resurgence of fine art, architecture, literature, and music
- the beginning of humanism as an intellectual movement.

Unlike medieval Christian theology, which emphasized the sinfulness of man, humanism was a secular movement that focused on the dignity and goodness of man. Humanists promoted the spread of knowledge and the cultivation of wisdom and focused on this life rather than the life imagined in the hereafter.

THE SCIENTIFIC REVOLUTION

The Scientific Revolution naturally grew out of the intellectual possibilities created by the expanding European worldview. Moreover, new inventions, such as compasses and telescopes, increased people's ability to investigate nature, and the printing press spread new ideas.

The first key event of the Scientific Revolution was the movement of human consciousness from a geocentric to a heliocentric understanding of the cosmos. Up until the sixteenth century, Europeans subscribed to the theories of Aristotle and Ptolemy in the realm of astronomy. Ptolemy, a second-century Greek astronomer, put Earth at the center of the universe and imagined each of the heavenly bodies he saw (i.e., the Sun and planets) in its own sphere, revolving around Earth, while the spheres themselves were nested, from Earth all the way up to the celestial region.

Polish mathematician and astronomer Nicolaus Copernicus first posited in 1514 that Earth and other planets revolved around the Sun—which was the center of the cosmos—and that the Moon revolved around Earth. He also hypothesized that the size and speed of each planet's orbit depended on its distance from the Sun. Copernicus waited to publish his final words on the matter of the heliocentric universe, fearing the wrath of Rome. In 1543, the year he died, he published *De Revolutionibus Orbium Coelestium* (*On the Revolutions of the Heavenly Spheres*). Not surprisingly, the

Copernicus formulated his heliocentric theory in 1514, but Greek astronomer Aristarchus of Samos (c. 310–230 BCE) also said Earth revolved around the Sun.

book was eventually banned by the Catholic Church.

Copernicus's work inspired other scientists to go further in their examination of the heavens. Tycho Brahe, a Danish astronomer, challenged Aristotle's notion of the unchanging harmony of the cosmos after he observed an exploding supernova and a comet during the 1570s. German astronomer Johannes Keppler used some of Brahe's data to show that planets moved around the Sun in elliptical orbits. But it would take the Italian mathematician Galileo Galilei to prove Copernicus's theories by observing the heavens through a telescope.

Galileo invented his own telescope, following the example of a Dutch lens grinder. He observed the moons of Jupiter, the rings of Saturn, the phases of Venus, and the surface of the Moon. He published his findings in 1610 and endorsed Copernicus's view of a heliocentric universe. Jupiter's moons proved that not all heavenly bodies revolved around Earth, while the phases of Venus showed that it was revolving around the Sun, not the Earth. In 1616, church authorities told Galileo he could not discuss or teach Copernican theory. Defying the order in 1632, Galileo published a staunch support of Copernicus's views in his *Dialogo sopra i Due Massimi Sistemi del Mondo, Tolemaico e Copernicano* (*Dialogue Concerning the Two Chief World Systems, Ptolemaic and Copernican*). Shortly thereafter he was called before the Inquisition and challenged on his heretical views. Galileo was forced to recant them (take them back), on pain

Legend has it that Galileo Galilei defied the Inquisition under his breath, saying "And yet it moves!" after being forced to deny the fact that Earth revolves around the Sun.

Galilée.

of torture and death. He gave in and was put under house arrest for the eight remaining years of his life.

The trial and sentencing of Galileo was the Catholic Church's last gasp against emerging empiricism—knowledge derived from sense experience—which would lead to additional scientific discoveries. No longer could organized religion hold back the floodgates of scientific discovery or legislate the boundaries of human knowledge and experience. Francis Bacon was born into this new world in 1561, destined to make his own contribution to the Scientific Revolution.

CHAPTER TWO

The Life of Francis Bacon

Born into a political family, Francis Bacon was groomed from an early age for public service. Queen Elizabeth I called him her "young Lord Keeper," a title his father, Sir Nicholas Bacon, held. The youngest son of Sir Nicholas, Francis was born on January 22, 1561, in London, England, three years before both Galileo and Shakespeare. His accomplished mother was proficient in Greek and Latin and also knew French and Italian. Her father had been the tutor to Edward VI, Elizabeth's half brother, who died in 1553, before he reached adulthood. Lady Anne Cooke Bacon reared her children in Calvinist Protestantism, which was a stricter form of Christianity than that of the Church of England. While Bacon would later criticize Protestant reformers, his desire to transform society reflected a Calvinist emphasis on an individual's social duties, while his unwavering loyalty to the Crown represented a Calvinist respect for the rule of law.

In Bacon's day, talented boys of the upper classes often began college at an early age. Bacon entered Trinity College at the age of twelve and studied for three years, living with his brother Anthony, two years his senior. Early on, Bacon took a dislike to the philosophy of Aristotle, prominent in curricula of the universities, and he left before taking a degree. He was sent to Paris by his father as a political apprentice to the English ambassador but was called back home when his father died in 1579. The sudden passing of his father left him no inheritance as the younger son of his father's second marriage, so he had to figure out a way to support himself. He entered Gray's Inn, a professional association for lawyers, studied to become an attorney, and gained admittance to the bar to practice law in 1582, at the age of twenty-one. Bacon had already embarked on his lifelong quest to curry favor with those in power.

BACON AND ELIZABETH I

Bacon had an uncle at court who was in a position to help him politically. Unfortunately, that uncle—Lord Burghley—did little to promote the fortunes of his nephew since he was too busy seeking advancement for his son Robert, a rival of his more talented cousin. Lord Burghley did help

Elizabeth I ruled England as its queen from 1558 to 1603. It was under her rule that England emerged as a major world power. This portrait of the queen dates from around 1588.

his nephew win a seat in Parliament in 1584, and Bacon continued to serve as a legislator, although he moved up to the House of Lords in 1617. Bacon generally supported the Crown's position, taking part in an investigation of English Catholics (who legally were not allowed to practice their religion) and supporting a harsh stance against Mary, Queen of Scots, who was seen as a threat to Elizabeth because some people—especially English Catholics—believed that Mary had a better claim to the English throne. In 1593, however, Bacon lost much of Elizabeth's patronage when, after she asked for funds from Parliament, Bacon insisted they be paid out over a period of six rather than three years. This stance put him at odds with Sir Walter Raleigh and his uncle. Bacon's balking in this matter of providing the queen money irreparably damaged his political prospects in Elizabeth's court.

Not even Bacon's friendship with Robert Devereux, the second Earl of Essex and a great favorite of the queen, could win him favor. The two men began their relationship as protégé and patron but soon became close friends. Essex tried to push Bacon forward, even as Elizabeth turned a deaf ear. Essex gave his friend a small estate worth about 1,800 pounds as a consolation. Elizabeth finally threw Bacon a bone in 1596, when he became her counsel extraordinary. Not long after, however, Bacon found himself in the difficult position of serving as one of the prosecuting lawyers against Essex after his friend was arrested for treason in 1601. Following Devereux's trial and exe-

Robert Devereux was a great favorite of Elizabeth I, but his violent, irrational temper erupted in a final treasonous act that cost him his life.

cution, Bacon was called upon to write a defense of the queen's actions in *A Declaration of the Practices & Treasons Attempted and Committed by Robert, Late Earle of Essex.* Essex was a popular figure, and many people were upset by his execution.

LITERARY CAREER

If politics was Bacon's livelihood, philosophy was his true calling. Bacon's chief interest was natural philosophy (what

BACON AND THE EARL OF ESSEX

Bacon has been vilified in some accounts of his life as being a heartless political sycophant (a "suck-up") who put his own advancement ahead of personal affection. In this vein, he has been faulted for playing a crucial role in the trial and subsequent execution of Robert Devereux. In his own time, Bacon sought to defend himself against public opinion after Queen Elizabeth's death in *Sir Francis Bacon His Apologie, in Certaine Imputations Concerning the Late Earle of Essex.*

Devereux was a young, handsome aristocrat who had arrived at court in his twenties and quickly became the queen's favorite. She gave him offices and a monopoly on the importation of sweet wines, a major source of income, but like many of the men around Elizabeth, the earl took too much for granted and underestimated the queen's ruthless courage. The brash and impetuous Devereux disobeyed military orders and on one occasion insulted Elizabeth, but she was persuaded to forgive him. In 1599, she sent him to Ireland to put down an uprising. He failed to do so and prematurely returned home, against orders. Essex was temporarily put under house arrest, and Elizabeth took away his lucrative wine monopoly. According to some sources, Bacon intervened with Elizabeth, and she again relented, lifting his house arrest. But according to other sources, Bacon had already abandoned his friend since he seemed ripe for a fall. In 1601, with a small contingent of armed men, Devereux tried but failed to incite the populace in an uprising against Elizabeth.

Throughout Essex's escalating disagreements with Elizabeth, Bacon repeatedly begged his friend to act with more discretion and warned him of the danger of challenging the queen. He also told Devereux that in a standoff with the queen, he was duty bound to take his sovereign's side. Moreover, as one of the queen's lawyers, Bacon would have had no choice but to prosecute her case against Devereux; to refuse would have been tantamount to treason.

today is called science), although he also delved into history and areas that modern scholars would call the social sciences. Bacon is praised today as an early philosopher of science and an important figure in the Scientific Revolution. He advocated for an empirical approach to science and the separation of science and religion. He famously wrote to Lord Burghley in 1592, "I have taken all of knowledge to be my province." In the preface to his great unfinished work, the *Instauratio Magna*, he wrote of his plan to fashion a scientific philosophy of practice: "Knowledge is power, not mere argument or ornament; it is not an opinion to be held ... but a work to be done; and I ... am laboring to lay the foundation not of any sect or doctrine, but of utility and power."

The first edition of his moral essays appeared in 1597, and a second book of essays, *De Sapientia Veterum* (*The Wisdom of the Ancients*), in 1609. In 1605, he published *The*

William Cecil (Lord Burghley), Queen Elizabeth 's most trusted advisor, was Francis Bacon's maternal uncle, although he wasn't much help in furthering his nephew's career at court.

Twoo Bookes of Francis Bacon. Of the Proficience and Advancement of Learning, Divine and Humane (generally known as *The Advancement of Learning*). Bacon had a grand plan to create a wide-ranging, encyclopedic work that covered many subjects but only completed two parts of this *Instauratio Magna* before he died. One was *De Dignitate et Augmentis Scientiarum* (often known by the shortened title *De Augmentis Scientiarum*), a revision and Latin translation of his earlier *The Advancement of Learning. De Augmentis Scientiarum* is the Latin translation of the earlier work's title, and the 1623 revision is sometimes referred to by the same English title (*The Advancement of Learning*) as the earlier work. The book surveys the sciences and enumerates a new classification of knowledge. The other was *Novum Organum*, which famously includes his challenge to Aristotelian induction and his own approach to the scientific method. These works were published in 1623 and 1620, respectively. Other important works include *Valerius Terminus: Of the Interpretation of Nature* (1603), which argues against mixing science and religion; *Historia Vitae et Mortis* (*The Historie of Life and Death*), a treatise on medicine; and *The New Atlantis* (1624), a futuristic fiction in which Bacon imagines a country run by scientists. Bacon also wrote a treatise on English common law, religious meditations, and other miscellaneous works of history, philosophy, and science.

PATRONAGE OF JAMES I

Bacon's fortunes turned when Elizabeth died and the Scottish king ascended the English throne as James I in 1603. Bacon became learned counsel the following year and worked on such issues as the union of Scotland and England and a middle road of religious tolerance of Catholics and nonconformist Protestant sects. He married Alice Barnhem, the fourteen-year-old daughter of a rich London businessman in 1606. As his star rose, he became attorney general in 1613, lord keeper of the seal (the same position his father had held) in 1617, and lord chancellor in 1618. The king also conferred titles on Bacon: Baron Verulam and Viscount St. Albans.

But Bacon seemed destined to stumble and fall politically, this time making enemies in Parliament by arguing against the abuse of monopolies. One of Bacon's offices was judge, and it was customary to accept gifts from people who were bringing suits before the court. Like everyone else, Bacon did not refuse these gifts. As a result, he was accused of bribery in 1621. The lord chancellor was promised some measure of protection from the king, and, thus, he fell on his sword, confessing to the charges. Bacon actually ruled against two of the petitioners in question, and none of his cases were ever retried. Nonetheless, he was found guilty by a parliamentary court and sentenced to indefinite imprisonment in the Tower of London and fined 40,000 pounds. He was also stripped of his public offices and forbidden from holding office in the future. Bacon ended up spending just a few days in jail, and the fine was withdrawn. In

After the death of Elizabeth I, James VI of Scotland became James I of England and Scotland. He patronized both Francis Bacon and William Shakespeare.

some ways, his disgrace was a "fortunate fall" since he devoted the rest of his life to scientific, philosophical, and literary pursuits. He died in April 1626 while performing an experiment to test the use of ice in preserving food.

CHAPTER THREE

The Classification of Knowledge

Francis Bacon intended to fish philosophy out of the swamp he believed it had sunk into because of the spread of Scholasticism's attempts to reconcile Aristotle with Christian theology. The sciences were stagnating, in his view, and he planned to create an intellectual edifice to rival Aristotle's with his *Instauratio Magna*. This work was never finished, but one of its completed sections was the *De Augmentis Scientiarum*, a revision and Latin translation of his *The Advancement of Learning* from 1605. Bacon translated his books of philosophy because he thought that Latin, the language of scholars of his time, would survive the test of time. He didn't have the same faith in English, which was a rapidly changing language during the English Renaissance. *De Augmentis Scientiarum* tackles faulty methods of learning and proposes a threefold classification of knowledge—history, the arts, and science—of which science is the most important part.

BACON'S JUSTIFICATION FOR SEEKING KNOWLEDGE

Bacon believed that man—being a creature of God—has a right to command nature but saw people of his time as being at the mercy of nature. Bacon argued that only science could open nature's book. In *De Augmentis Scientiarum*, he writes that it is necessary to "make the circuit of knowledge, noticing what parts lie waste and uncultivated, and abandoned by the industry of man, with a view to engage, by a faithful mapping out of the deserted tracks, the energies of public and private persons in their improvement." Bacon means he will determine which areas of learning have been ignored and then figure out how people can collectively work together to improve its advancement.

Bacon justifies his undertaking by refuting the idea, which can be found in the Bible, that human beings should not pursue knowledge. "It was not the pure knowledge of nature ... that occasioned the fall; but the proud knowledge of good and evil, with an intent in man to give law to himself, and depend no more upon God," Bacon says. He also argues that, while superficial knowledge of philosophy may turn a mind to atheism, a fuller understanding will return a person to religion. Thus, he urges man to not limit his searching,

This title page to an English translation of *De Augmentis Scientiarum* (1640) pictures Bacon's metaphor of knowledge as a ship that travels through the seas of time.

either in "the book of God's word" or in his works. The investigation of nature is both a right and duty and does not contradict obligations to religion.

ERRORS OF LEARNING

To advance learning, however, it is first necessary to understand the errors that get in the way of study. The learned sometimes fall into the error of putting eloquence (speaking well) ahead of content and thus pay more attention to their choice of words and phrases than to the "weight of matter" they are discussing. Further, if they worship their own minds and understanding and go too far into contemplation (thinking deeply about philosophy), even while withdrawing from nature and the observations of their experience, they are not likely to advance learning.

Another error of learning is to rush to judgment. "If we begin with certainties, we shall end in doubts; but if we begin with doubts, and are patient in them, we shall end in certainties," Bacon says. After all, the purpose of knowledge is to generate something concrete that will have a good purpose for humankind. Bacon's method of inductive inquiry, which he expands upon in *Novum Organum*, begins not with a certainty or even a hypothesis, but rather starts with investigation.

THE PURPOSE OF LEARNING

Human learning inspires us to glorify God and is a corrective against atheism and error, according to Bacon. Knowledge tames the "barbarity and fierceness of men's minds" and curbs the tendencies of frivolity (or light-mindedness) and excessive egoism. Moreover, knowledge teaches us to examine all sides of a question and accept nothing unless we test its veracity. The greatest power on earth is knowledge and learning. Through knowledge we surpass all other creatures. Bacon equates knowledge and learning with immortality, in that our knowledge lives beyond us, passed from generation to generation. Such knowledge is more than a mere image of the past since it has the capacity to generate seeds in the minds of others, provoking and causing "infinite actions and opinions in succeeding ages." Bacon compares knowledge to a ship that carries riches even to the remotest of regions; likewise, the ship of knowledge passes through the seas of time with the treasure of previous generations.

The rulers of the world have a responsibility to safeguard this treasure of mankind, in books and halls of learning and among learned people. Bacon then critiques the educational institutions of his day, saying that colleges are dedicated only to professions, not more generally to the arts and sciences, which hinders the progress of learning. Moreover, the overemphasis on professional learning has had a negative effect on the growth of the sciences and even on states and governments. The sciences suffer, not only for lack of educational institutions, but also for lack of instruments. Bacon advocates for tools as well as material to experiment on. He also points to a lack of practicums, in which students would

Bacon's loss of political favor gave him more time to devote to writing in the last five years of his life, in which he published *De Augmentis Scientiarum*.

actually apply knowledge, in universities.

PARTS OF HUMAN LEARNING

Bacon divides understanding into memory (history), imagination (poesy, or the arts), and reason (philosophy, or the sciences). He points out that while some books existed about the "mechanical arts," such as agriculture, this learning was considered inferior when, in fact, it is the kind of information that can be most counted on. In Bacon's view, the mechanical arts are most fundamental for natural philosophy (science) and likely to provide the most benefit to mankind. In this part of his critique, Bacon is moving toward an empirical approach to knowledge. He advocates a nuts-and-bolts, cause-and-effect view of nature and the world that is based on observation and analysis.

Bacon segments philosophy into divine philosophy, natural philosophy, and human philosophy (what we now call the social sciences). Divine philosophy may be studied by observing God's creatures. But Bacon says that extreme prejudice results when religion and philosophy are mixed. He is in favor of their separation "because a mixture of these makes both a heretical religion and a fantastic and superstitious philosophy." Here is the first call in European philosophy for a clear separation between the religious and the secular, for the purpose of advancing science.

Natural philosophy needs both miners and smiths, according to another of Bacon's metaphors.

Some must dig, while some must refine and hammer. To put it more literally, some must speculate and some must put philosophy into practice. Thus, natural philosophy includes both physics and metaphysics. Physics inquires into material causes, while metaphysics is focused on formal and final causes. Mathematics is also assigned to natural philosophy. Pure mathematics includes geometry and arithmetic, which are necessary to such fields of study as perspective, music, astronomy, architecture, and engineering, to name a few.

Self-knowledge is also assigned to the realm of natural philosophy since human beings are a part of nature. Medicine is also in this realm: knowledge concerning the body includes health, beauty, strength, and pleasure. This coincides with medicine's knowledge of cure, decoration (cosmetics), activity (athletics), and voluptuary (sensual pleasure). Bacon faults medicine for not progressing and points out that modern practitioners failed to do what Hippocrates did, which was to keep a narrative of their cases and their outcomes, which can help direct future judgments of illness and treatment. A comprehensive study of anatomy is also lacking. He believes that doctors should be allowed to help death along through the practice of euthanasia, when people are in great pain and near their end.

BACON'S PSYCHOLOGICAL INSIGHTS

Bacon notes that many external factors affect the way people

Hippocrates (c. 450–380 BCE) is credited with writing the first professional code of ethics for physicians. Scholars now think his *Corpus Hippocraticum* may have been the work of several authors.

think. Further, he contradicts Aristotle's assumption that natural inclinations cannot be trained by the will:

> **We come now to those things which are within our own power, and work upon the mind, and affect and govern the will and the appetite; whence they have great efficacy in altering the manners. And here philosophers should diligently inquire into the powers and energy of custom, exercise, habit, education, example, imitation, emulation, company, friendship, praise, reproof, exhortation, reputation, laws, books, studies, etc.; for these are the things which reign in men's morals. By these agents the mind is formed and subdued; and of these ingredients remedies are prepared, which, so far as human means can reach, conduce to the preservation and recovery of the health of the mind.**

Aristotle claimed that culture ("custom") could not change people's natural tendencies, but Bacon argues that this is easily proved false and gives two examples—the training of the voice to be more pleasing to the ear and acclimation to degrees of heat and cold. Thus, it is possible to cultivate habits of both body and mind.

SUMMARY

De Augmentis Scientiarum throws down the gauntlet, chal-

BACON ON EUTHANASIA

Bacon became the first person to use the word "euthanasia" in a medical context in the second chapter of the fourth book of *De Augmentis Scientiarum.* He writes:

> **And further, we esteem it the office of a physician to mitigate the pains and tortures of diseases, as well as to restore health; and this not only when such a mitigation, as of a dangerous symptom, may conduce to recovery; but also, when there being no further hopes of recovery, it can only serve to make the passage out of life more calm and easy.**
>
> **But the physicians of our times make a scruple of attending the patient after the disease is thought past cure, though, in my judgment, if they were not wanting to their own profession and to humanity itself, they should here give their attendance to improve their skill, and make the dying person depart with greater ease and tranquility. We therefore set down as deficient an inquiry after a method of relieving the agonies of the dying, calling it by the name of euthanasia exteriori, to distinguish it from the internal composure, procured to the soul in death.**

lenging the received ideas of the ancients and proposing a new classification of knowledge that stresses a practical approach to science. The first of Bacon's texts on the philosophy of science, it highlights the importance of observation (empiricism) in advancing the cause of knowledge and introduces ideas that are further elaborated on in *Novum Organum, Sylva Sylvarum* (an unfinished text on natural history), and *The New Atlantis.*

CHAPTER FOUR

BACON'S NEW METHOD

In *Novum Organum*, Francis Bacon lays out a new method of doing science that opposes the Scholastics and their understanding of Aristotle. The *Organon* was the name given to Aristotle's six works on logic. Bacon, along with the other philosophers who followed Aristotle, benefited from his principles of logic, which are still in use today. However, Bacon objected to the use of logic by itself to discover new scientific principles or advance the agenda of science. The Scholastics had made Aristotle's logic the basis of their epistemology (theory of knowledge) to the exclusion of the observation of nature. Bacon also objected to the telos (goal or final end) of Scholastic philosophy, which was to perfect deductive reasoning and present the strongest argument. For Bacon, the telos of science was to penetrate the secrets of nature and obtain practical results that would benefit mankind.

The ship of knowledge (also pictured on the title page of *Novum Organum*) carries treasures from age to age, but false ideas must be thrown overboard.

A NEW EPISTEMOLOGY

The preface of *Novum Organum* begins by asserting that those who think they understand the laws of nature do science and philosophy a great disservice. By spreading such a belief, they put an end to inquiry. On the other hand, those who believe that nothing can be known have gone too far. The ancient Greeks, whose writings are lost to the West, took a position between these two extremes. They tried to engage with nature but put too much trust in their own understanding and applied no rules to their study. After making this argument, Bacon introduces his own method. It is to "establish progressive stages of certainty," which begin with the senses. Nonetheless, the senses are to be "helped and guarded by a certain process of correction." When people need to move a heavy object, they do not rely on brute force but instead use mechanical instruments. So too, when investigating nature, people cannot rely entirely on their "naked intellect."

Human beings can know only what they observe in nature, but understanding requires instruments of both the hand and the mind. While the productions of the mind seem numerous, in fact they derive from only a few things that are known. These known facts are mostly arrived at by chance rather than science. Bacon says that the science of his day consists of systems for ordering phenomena, with no method for inventing new things.

So why do people know so little? While the senses may seem subtle, nature is far subtler, Bacon says. Thus, much of what people observe is misunderstood. Things are not apparent from observation alone. Here is an example of nature's subtlety—although one that would have been unknown to Bacon: The earth doesn't feel like it's moving, yet it is spinning on its axis at about 1,000 miles per hour (1,600 km/h) and orbiting the sun at 18.5 miles per second (30 km/s). Bacon says current science (the science of his time) and logic are useless in uncovering new truths about nature. What he means is that logic cannot advance arguments based on false premises or wrong ideas. For science, we need to establish first principles, Bacon says. According to Aristotle, a first principle is the first basis by which we know some-

Aristotle, one of the greatest of the Greek philosophers, was rediscovered by medieval Christians who attempted to reconcile his ideas with Christian theology.

thing. Some examples include logic itself or an element, like fire or water. In other words, a first principle is something that seems indisputable and self-evident.

Classical logic works by syllogism, a method of reasoning in which a conclusion is drawn based on two propositions that share a "term" with the conclusion. The propositions or premises must also share a common "middle term" not present in the conclusion. The following is an example of a syllogism: all children have mothers; all mothers conceive with sperm from biological fathers; therefore, all children have biological fathers. The first two premises share the term "mothers," and the conclusion shares the term "children" with the first premise and "biological fathers" with the second premise. But a logical syllogism can also result in a falsehood. For instance, all killer dogs have long, sharp teeth. Your pet dog had long, sharp teeth. Thus, your beloved pet is a killer. It is easy to see how logic by itself is useless for science unless it is applied to careful, repeated observation and experiment.

In Bacon's view, the truth can be uncovered in only two ways: the first method moves away from perception and the senses and toward general axioms. Axioms are accepted or seemingly self-evident principles. From these general axioms, judgments are formed and "middle axioms" are then discovered. In the second method, axioms are "derived from the senses and particulars, rising by a gradual and unbroken ascent" until a general axiom can be fashioned. Bacon prefers the second method. It can be equated with inductive reasoning, while the first method is equivalent to deduction. For scientific inquiry, Bacon wishes to avoid deduction, which begins with a hypothesis or assumption. He calls deduction Anticipations of Nature. He calls induction, which is arrived at through considering the facts in a methodical process before arriving at a conclusion, Interpretation of Nature.

ROOTING OUT THE IDOLS

Before scientists can correctly use their powers of observation to make discoveries or correctly apply logic, they must first purge themselves of idols. The meaning of "idols" for Bacon is equivalent to false images or notions, which he says are deeply rooted in the mind and have taken hold of human understanding. The idols are four: Idols of the Tribe, Idols of the Cave, Idols of the Marketplace, and Idols of the Theater.

The Idols of the Tribe are the most numerous and pervasive since they are based in human nature. The tribe refers to the family of humankind. All sense perceptions are limited "according to the measure of the individual," and Bacon compares human understanding to a "false mirror" that distorts reality and integrates sense perceptions with our internal nature or mind.

We naturally want to impose an order on existence, whether it exists or not. We tend to see parallels and similarities that do not exist. It is natural for us to

immediately notice facts that support an opinion we have adopted, even if there is more evidence contradicting rather than affirming our opinion. Bacon provides the example of someone who prays to a deity to avoid a shipwreck and then claims their prayers were answered, without considering the many prayers to avoid misfortune that apparently go unanswered. A similar example would be people comforting themselves by saying that "things happen for a reason," when no apparent reason exists for some misfortune that has just been suffered. Bacon puts all superstition—including dreams, omens, astrology, and divine judgment—in this category, saying that we delight in such vanities. They are vanities because we imagine the universe is contriving events especially for our benefit. We react more emotionally to positive than to negative events, although it would be best to have detachment toward both for the purpose of scientific exploration.

Human understanding is also at the mercy of ideas that enter the mind suddenly and arouse the

Francis Bacon notes people swear by many irrational belief systems that have no basis in fact. Two such systems that survive until today are fortune telling and astrology.

imagination. Moreover, the mind never rests, so we cannot conceive an end to the world and are predisposed to think there is something "beyond," which leads us to search for causes "prior in the order of nature." In struggling toward final causes related to "the nature of man" rather than "the nature of the universe" (that is

IDOLS OF THE CAVE, MARKETPLACE, AND THEATER

Bacon briefly covers the remaining idols that cast a shadow on clear perception and thinking.

Idols of the Cave: Each individual man or woman has his or her own personal idols, which reside in a personal cave. The distortion may be due to peculiarities of personality, education, or environment. People may become attached to a particular idea they have invented or to which they have become habituated. Bacon accuses Aristotle of harboring this idol, making "natural philosophy a mere bond servant of logic, thereby rendering it contentious and well-nigh useless."

Idols of the Marketplace: Commerce and interaction among people are responsible for these idols. The wrong use of words can confuse a person's understanding and lead him or her into "empty controversies and idle fancies." Bacon points out that "words stand in the way and resist … change." Idols imposed by words are either names of things that don't exist or names of things that are confused or poorly defined. The kind of idol is more dangerous and harder to root out since it incorporates some semblance of truth and thus can quite easily lead people astray.

Idols of the Theater: These idols come from received systems of belief or philosophies or from "wrong laws of demonstration." Bacon calls these idols "stage plays, representing worlds of their own creation after an unreal and scenic fashion." These idols can be entire systems or principles of science that have come to be accepted as true, even though they have no basis in reality.

sensory experience), we will likely create a "defiled" philosophy.

The mind prefers to alight on what is pleasant and what it would like to be true. Thus, people reject what is difficult, serious, or requires a lot of work. Superstition, arrogance, pride, deference to common opinion, and many other factors can "color and infect" the understanding, often in ways that go unnoticed by the perceiver.

SUMMARY

The difficulties in making headway in the sciences can be laid at the door of bad philosophy and distorted perception. First, it will not be possible to make new discoveries in science by beginning with faulty assumptions. These faulty anticipations result from Aristotelian Scholasticism and the widespread use of deduction to solve problems of logic that have become far removed from nature. Second, it is necessary to start from scratch when it comes to thinking, but a clean slate requires the purging of the idols so that the aspiring scientist or natural philosopher can see as clearly as possible what he or she is looking at, with a minimum of bias. In the second book of his *Novum Organum*, Bacon details his method of induction.

CHAPTER FIVE

A NEW APPROACH TO INDUCTION

Francis Bacon is sometimes wrongly credited with inventing the scientific method. In fact, some form of the method has been in existence since human beings first emerged from the forest and began to reason. In the recorded history of Western civilization, the scientific method can be said to begin with Aristotle (384–322 BCE), the most famous of the Greek philosophers who incorporated both induction and deduction into his system of logic. Roger Bacon (1214–1294 CE), a medieval English philosopher of science well versed in both Aristotle's logic and the writings of Muslim scientists on optics, advocated for a scientific method that included observation, hypothesis, experimentation, and verification. William of Ockham (1287–1347; also spelled Occam) made an important contribution to the scientific method

Roger Bacon was a Franciscan friar, natural philosopher, and early supporter of the scientific method. He knew the works of Aristotle and the Middle-Eastern scientist Alhazen.

with the principles of parsimony and plurality, which came to be known as Occam's razor. Occam's razor boils down to the idea that the simplest explanation is usually the right one. Contemporaneous with Francis Bacon was Galileo in Italy (1564–1642), who practiced his own version of the scientific method, involving observation, hypothesis, experimentation, and the use of mathematics. Francis Bacon advocated a scientific method based on inductive rather than deductive reasoning. He is important to the history of science for stressing the necessity of observation in drawing conclusions and for championing an empiricist approach to science. Empiricism is an epistemological theory that argues that all knowledge is arrived at through sense experience.

BACON'S METHOD

Bacon explains his approach to the scientific method in the second part of *Novum Organum.* His method stresses induction. This is a style of reasoning that begins with collecting related facts on a particular subject and then drawing a hypothesis. Deduction is the opposite; it begins with a hypothesis and then collects the facts that prove it.

Bacon's inductive method differs from classical induction in that it eliminates possible hypotheses or explanations (exclusion) as it goes along and is not just simple enumeration of a series of facts. While Aristotle primarily relies on deduction, he says that induction is a progression from particulars to a universal. Bacon points out that the problem with classical induction is that if a general axiom proves false, all intermediate axioms may be false as well. For example, suppose that, after observing a half dozen flowers identified as annuals, a scientist concludes that such blooms will always die at the end of the season. The scientist further surmises that all flowers identified as annuals will need to be replanted. But, in fact, pansies as well as other flowers identified as annuals will bloom for a second season or more. Thus, the conclusion will prove to be incorrect, and statements (intermediate axioms) about individual annuals may also be incorrect.

Philosophers did not thoroughly examine the problem of induction—the impossibility of accounting for every single instance before drawing a conclusion—until David Hume (1711–1766) squarely faced the limitations of empiricism. But Bacon understood more about the problem of induction than Aristotle. For this reason, Bacon recommends moving slowly from one proposition or generalization—called an axiom—to the next in a stepwise fashion, testing each proposition through observation and experiment. Each axiom is a step on the ladder toward a higher truth. Bacon's induction starts with sensory data and progresses from lower certainties to higher certainties. It can also move back and forth between middle to higher propositions. By progressively crossing off hypotheses as the ladder of induction is climbed, the scientist gets to a point where only one logical explana-

Eighteenth-century philosopher David Hume reached the limits of empiricism by arguing that all people could know with certainty was their own perceptions.

tion remains. Bacon's methodical elimination of false hypotheses and ferreting out of exceptions and negative instances results in a complex base of knowledge, supported by observed facts or empirical data. Bacon also emphasizes the importance of never generalizing beyond what the facts indicate.

The method Bacon conceived for carrying out induction was to use a series of tables to consider propositions. In *Novum Organum*, he used the property of heat to demonstrate his inductive tables. The first table of induction lists as many instances as possible of conditions in which heat occurs. The second table lists conditions under which heat is not present. The third table looks at the degree of heat present under varying conditions. After these tables are examined and analyzed, Bacon can then draw his first conclusion (hypothesis) about the nature of the property being examined. Bacon calls this the First Vintage. The second stage of induction focuses on exclusion. Once again, tables of presence and absence are set up, and research is done to discover the relationship between heat and a series of other qualities. Clearly, Bacon has not thrown out the baby of deduction with the bathwater of sloppy Aristotelian generalization. Instead Bacon's method of induction consists of forming tentative hypotheses along the way as he moves toward a final hypothesis. This method is an improvement, but, as his critics point out, when does the scientist know enough instances have been observed and examined?

THE SCIENTIFIC METHOD TODAY

How much modern scientists use Bacon's approach to the scientific method is to some extent a matter of opinion. Moreover, research and experimentation in science differs, to some degree, by field. While it is certainly true that scientists nowadays rely on a working hypothesis (deduction), they certainly use induction, examining data from which they draw conclusions.

Today's scientific method is described in a number of ways, and sources differ about the number of steps involved. The scientific method generally involves these steps, which can be further broken down:

- Observation and description of a phenomenon, or object of perception
- Formulation of a hypothesis to either explain the phenomenon, predict the existence of other phenomena in relation to the first thing being observed, or predict the interaction of the phenomenon with other phenomena
- Creation and carrying out of experiments to test predictions and assumptions
- Presentation of results that either prove or disprove the hypothesis or point in the direction for further investigation.

The scientific method is used to sequence the genomes of plants, information used to breed varieties that are more hardy or resistant to adverse growing conditions.

TESTING THE HYPOTHESIS

Experiments involve a number of repetitions, often done under varying conditions. The scientific method requires that experimental results bear out the predictions of the hypothesis. If they do not, the hypothesis must be thrown

out or modified. For example, when Alexander Fleming first noticed that the bacteria he had been growing in a discarded petri dish in 1928 was killed by a mold that had appeared in the same dish, he hypothesized that the mold had an antibacterial property. But the first antibiotic was not produced until scientists had run repeated experiments in petri dishes and, later, on lab mice injected with bacteria and penicillin. It was only at that point that they finally had enough evidence of penicillin's antibacterial properties. Penicillin was not manufactured as an antibiotic drug until 1942.

In some types of scientific experiments, control groups are used to correct for human error (which can be introduced through bias, either on the part of the scientist or the subject). This is because what people think or feel about phenomena can affect that phenomena and bias can affect an experimental result. For example, the placebo effect refers to how people's belief in a treatment can positively affect how they respond to it, independent of the treatment's medical efficacy. When scientists test new medicines, they always use a control group that is made

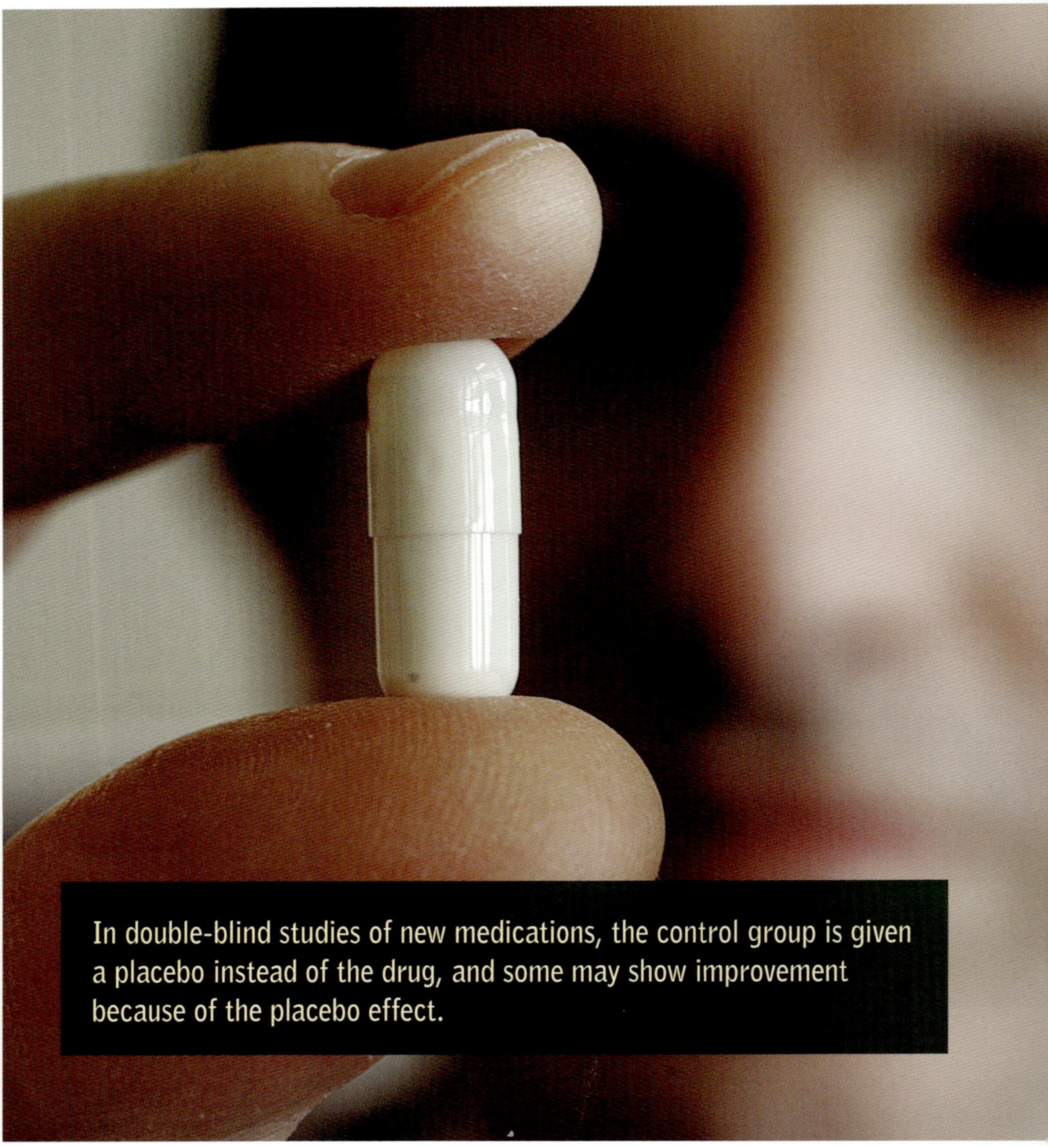

In double-blind studies of new medications, the control group is given a placebo instead of the drug, and some may show improvement because of the placebo effect.

up of people who get a placebo instead of the medicine. Neither the people in the drug study nor the scientists themselves know which group is taking the medicine.

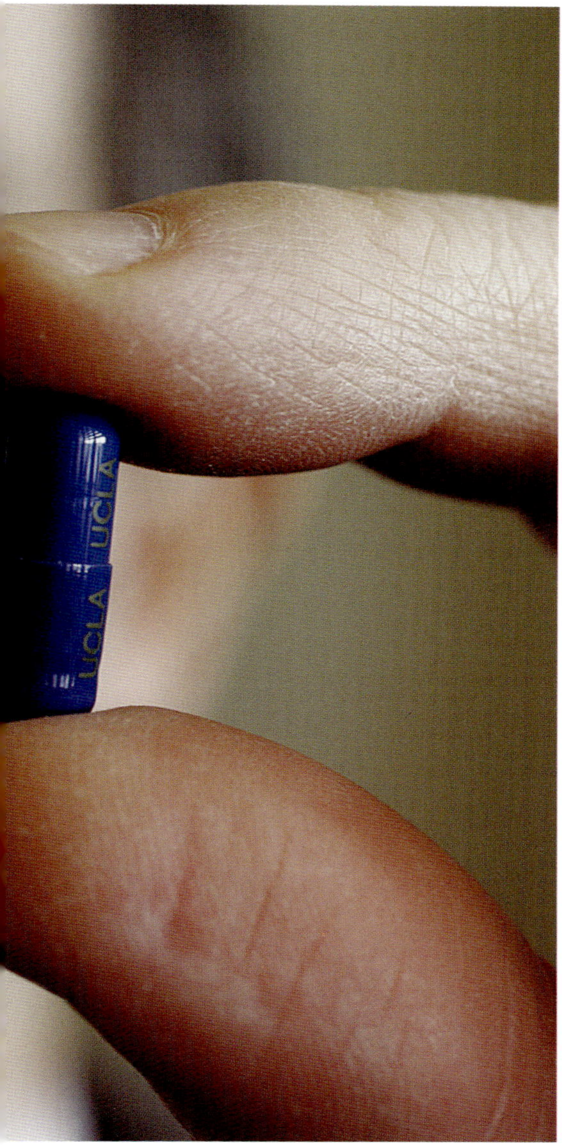

This approach ensures that people's biases do not affect results.

SUMMARY

Although scientists nowadays begin any experiment with a hypothesis, there is no doubt that observations are an essential part of any scientific endeavor. Although scientists do not methodically pile up instances in which they observe a phenomenon before drawing a hypothesis, as recommended by Bacon, they do use both inductive and deductive logic. And certainly, before a scientist formulates a hypothesis, they make preliminary observations of a phenomenon. If they did not, they could not have an idea about anything. The extent and methods of direct observation of phenomena depend on the field of study. For example, a physicist cannot directly observe particles the way a biologist can observe plants, animals, or

POPPER'S THEORY OF FALSIFICATION

Falsification of the hypothesis was an idea introduced to the scientific method by the philosopher Karl Popper in the late twentieth century. Popper was mostly concerned with the "pseudo-sciences"—meaning social sciences in which practitioners pile up instances of a particular type of phenomena in support of a particular theory that is not necessarily based in fact. For example, according to Sigmund Freud's personality theory in the field of psychoanalysis, the personality is organized by three principles with different agendas: the ego, the id, and the superego. But there is no way to prove or disprove such a theory.

Popper argued that true scientists could attempt to falsify their hypotheses to ensure they were true. The classic example of falsification provided by Popper is the black swan, found only in Australia, which proves that not all swans are white. In the social sciences, it is generally not possible to falsify a theory. This marks the difference between science and pseudoscience, in Popper's view. Although Popper criticized induction with his method of falsification, Bacon actually anticipated Popper's ideas when he said in *Novum Organum* that it is necessary to methodically eliminate false hypotheses.

even microorganisms. Thus, physicists use mathematical calculations to study particles that cannot be seen but whose nature can be observed through their behavior in lab experiments, with the use of complex machinery such as particle accelerators.

CHAPTER SIX

The New Atlantis

Francis Bacon never completed his utopian novel, *The New Atlantis*, which was first published as a fragment in 1624, but his utopian fantasy made its mark on both science and culture. The British Royal Society, founded in 1660 to promote scientific inquiry, took Bacon's vision of a society based in science as its inspiration. This work influenced and expressed the aspirations of Renaissance culture. The men of the Renaissance sought to free Europe from medievaism and create a society in which secular science might flourish. *The New Atlantis* was remarkably prescient in guessing at areas of scientific advancement and predicting the increasingly dominant role science would play in organizing society.

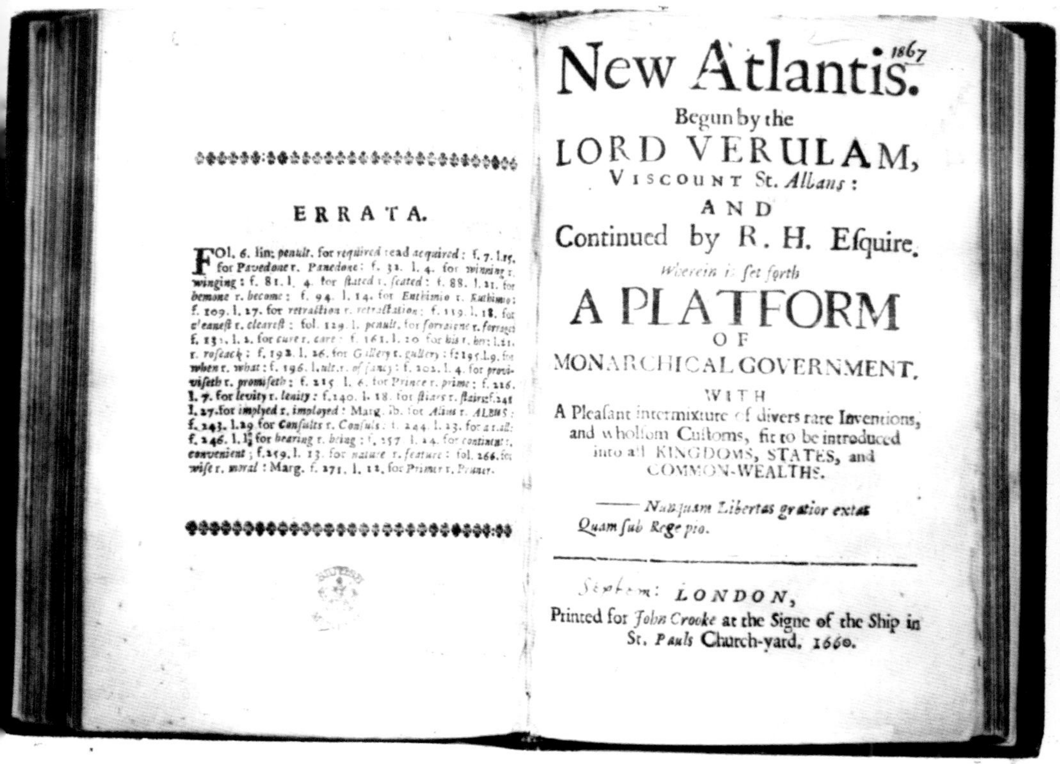

The New Atlantis is a fragment of science fiction created by Francis Bacon in which he envisioned a utopian society ruled by benevolent natural philosophers (scientists).

THE BACK STORY

In Bacon's fable, a crew of explorers sails from Peru, headed to China and Japan by way of "the South Sea." As often happens in shipwreck stories, the wind-powered boat is becalmed for weeks, and then wracked by storms that knock it off course. The crew is in danger of starving to death.

Luckily, they sight land and are received on a mysterious island by highly intelligent men dressed in beautiful clothing. They are told they may stay on the island only long enough to recover (some of the crew is sick). Later they are allowed to stay indefinitely, once the residents of this place, called Bensalem, realize the crew is Christian. During their stay, they learn about the island and its inhabitants. They discover that the island became Christian some twenty years after the resurrection of Jesus (which, according to Christian doctrine, would mean the island's residents converted around 50 CE). Through a miracle that involved the intervention of a wise man, the residents were given an ark containing the complete biblical scriptures (the Hebrew Scriptures and the New Testament), including parts of the New Testament that had not yet been written by that time! Thus, the residents practice a form of pure Christianity that has not been tainted by the history of Europe.

Soon the guests begin meeting various representatives of Bensalem and learn the people's customs. The guests are also given a history lesson. Apparently there was a time in the distant past when worldwide navigation was much more advanced and the people of Bensalem traded with people from many nations, including Atlantis. This mythical land with an advanced society first appears in the writings of Plato, a Greek philosopher who preceded Aristotle. After Atlantis (which Europeans of Bacon's era located in the Americas) was destroyed, Bensalem lost contact with the rest of the Americas. Some time later—about 1,900 years before the shipwrecked crew landed there—a wise ruler decided to cut off communication with the rest of the world to save his people from the corruption of outsiders. This king, named Solamona, established a patriarchal utopia (a "perfect" society run by men). One important custom is to honor the patriarchs who have thirty living members in their line with a Feast of the Family. Also established by this revered lawgiver is Salomon's House, which "is dedicated to the study of the works and creatures of God." The visitors' guide points out the similarities between Solamona and the wise King Solomon of the Bible (who the guide claims wrote a natural history of plants that had been lost to the rest of the world outside Bensalem). This scientific society, sometimes called the College of the Six Days Works (in reference to the six days God took to complete the creation), is the seat of government for Bensalem. King Solamona also decreed that the only people who will leave the island are hand-picked wise men ("brethren" of Salomon's House) who travel to distant lands every twelve years to glean the best of humanity's advances in other societies and bring them back home. These explorers work undercover so they are never known to the outside world.

SALOMON'S HOUSE

After some days have passed, the sailors receive the honor of a visit with one of the Fathers of Salomon's House, who

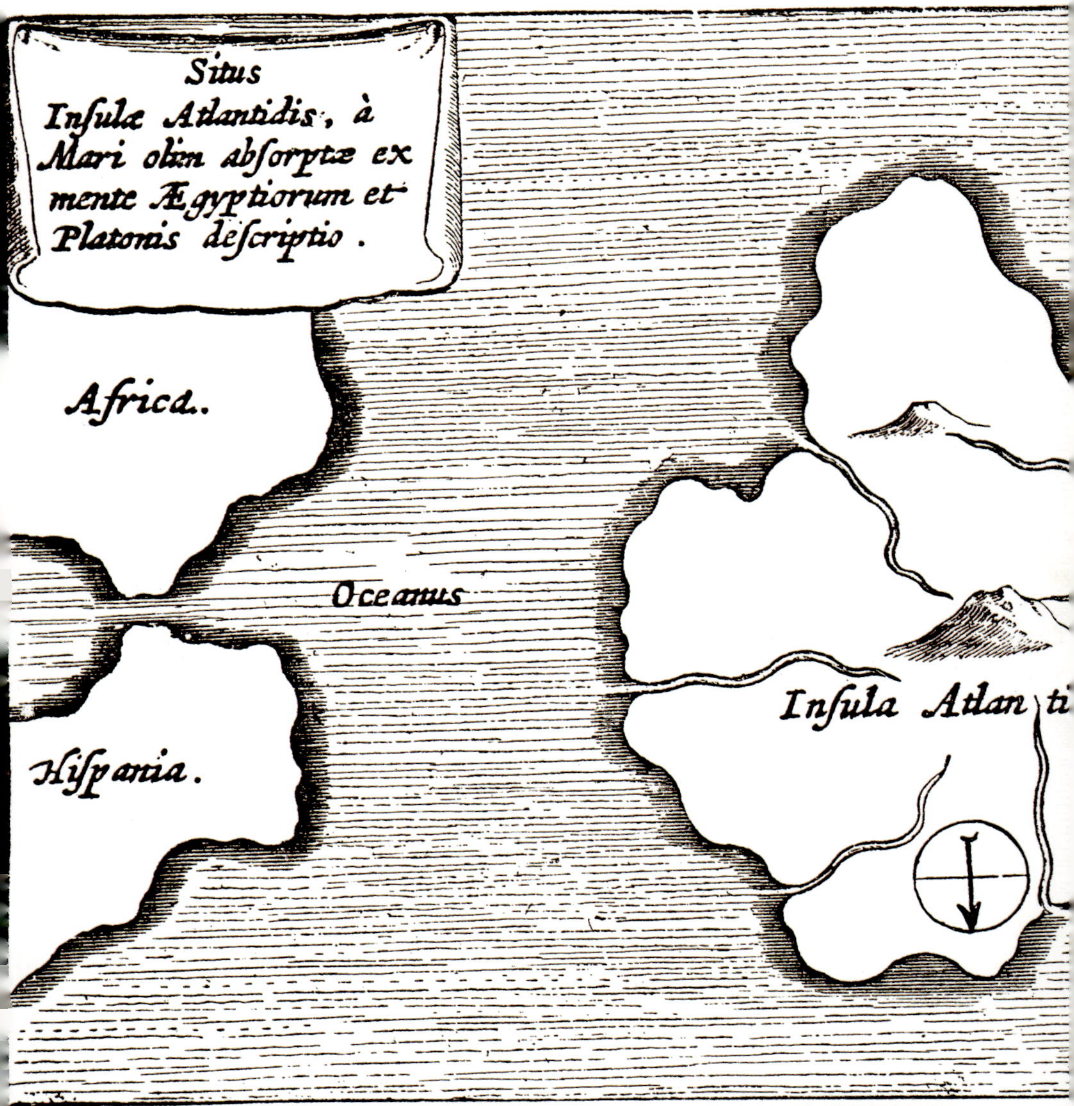

The legend of Atlantis began with Plato, who said it had been an island in the Atlantic Ocean. Europeans of Bacon's time located it in the Americas.

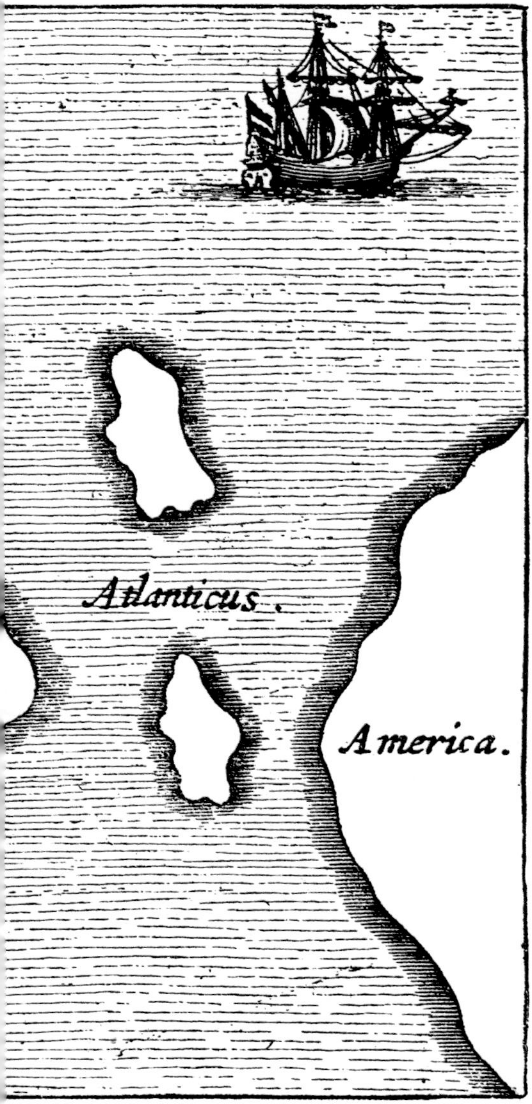

explains how the house of science works. "The end of our foundation is the knowledge of causes," the Father says, "and secret motion of things; and the enlarging of the bounds of human empire, to the effecting of all things possible."

The house has upper, lower, and middle realms—caves and mines, mountains, open stretches of land, towers, and all manner of man-made structures, as well as natural structures that have been fashioned by man. The scientists at Salomon's House carry out experiments on all aspects of nature. They are sorted into groups by job, and each has a job title. For example, the travelers who bring back knowledge from other realms are called Merchants of Light. Those who collect the experiments in books are Depredators, while those

The name of King Solomon in the Hebrew Scriptures is synonymous with wisdom, which is why Bacon invokes him in his tale of a wise ruler with a similar name.

who try new experiments are called Pioneers or Miners. Those who find practical uses for what is learned through experiments are called Dowry-men or Benefactors. Not all the work of the house is shared with the public, and the scientists decide what to release and what to keep secret.

The Father also tells the sailor-guests that the brotherhood has "certain hymns and services," in which they thank God for his "marvelous works" and ask his aid and blessing. Finally, the fragment ends with the Father from Salomon's House telling the sailors that the scientists are in charge of declaring when catastrophic events will occur—such as disease, plagues, floods, and so forth. They also provide advice about how to prevent, remedy, or cope with various types of problems caused by nature.

APPLYING BACON'S VISION: A HOUSE OF SCIENCE

The founders of the Royal Society—an academy of science that was founded in London—were followers of Bacon. They first met to hear an astronomy lecture by Christopher Wren, a highly respected architect who designed more than fifty of London's churches, including St. Paul's Cathedral. Inspired by the ideas of Bacon—and especially fired up by his notion of an institute of scientists—they resolved to create an informal college of experimental learning in mathematics and natural philosophy. They agreed to meet weekly

IN SALOMON'S HOUSE

Here are some of the scientific activities carried out by the wise men of Bensalem, according to Bacon's utopian tale:

- Observe natural events, such as meteors and weather
- Experiment with different types of burial to see its effect on what is buried
- Engage in what modern scientists call genetic engineering (scientists change the nature of plants and species, growing things smaller and larger than normal and mixing species)
- Create weather events
- Dissect and experiment on all types of animals without restraint
- Create drugs and other medicines
- View objects through telescopes and microscopes (using "the glasses and means to see small and minute bodies perfectly and distinctly," including what is in "urine and blood")
- Experiment with sound
- Prepare "engines and instruments for all sorts of motion"

to discuss scientific topics and observe experiments done by various group members. The Royal Society received a charter from the English king, Charles II, in 1662. The charter gave the Royal Society an institutional structure and royal patronage, although it always remained an independent and private organization. The first written account of its work was published in 1667. The cover of this publication showed the king, with Sir Francis Bacon sitting on his left and the organization's first president (William Brouncker, a mathematician) sitting on his right.

The society saw itself as a research organization and clearinghouse for new information. The oldest scientific institute in the world, it was also the first to create a process for publishing peer-reviewed scientific papers. Its flagship publication, *Philosophical Transactions*, was established in 1665 and adopted by the society in 1753. This publication is the oldest continually published scientific journal in the world. Since the first scientific society was established by Englishmen, English became the language of science—and even today is widely used to discuss and disseminate scientific ideas.

Many famous scientists have been members of the Royal Society. For example, the mathematician Sir Isaac Newton, the father of classical physics, was president of the society from 1703 to 1727. In the modern era, many of the society's members are Nobel Prize winners.

Sir Isaac Newton—known for his work on gravity, calculus, the laws of motion, optics, and more—was an early president of the Royal Society.

SUMMARY

The New Atlantis is remarkable for the fact that it predicted modern scientific research centers and anticipated the idea of an international scientific community that carries out peer review and advances the agenda of progress. Today scientists publish findings and share results. Bacon imagined a government that would subsidize science, and, indeed, much scientific research gets public funding. Also remarkable is that many of Bacon's imaginings are now reality—genetic engineering, advanced optics in telescopes and microscopes, and widespread animal experimentation. *The New Atlantis* has been parsed by critics who both admire and loathe it: some see Bacon's dream as a beacon that shone a light on the future miracles of Western science, while others see it as the preamble to the historic and ongoing desecration of nature.

CHAPTER SEVEN

Bacon's Legacy: Making Nature an Instrument of Man

The Western idea that man is the predominant creature on Earth and has a right to use all the other creatures and nature itself for his own benefit is strongly associated with Francis Bacon, the first spokesman for scientific progress. This is not to say that he was the first one to have this idea; Bacon should be viewed as a product of Western culture and an embodiment of his cultural milieu. Yet he has iconic status as the first philosopher of modern science, and his view is that nature should be understood and conquered. This outlook has allowed humanity to make life much easier and more enjoyable for many people and has rapidly accelerated the growth of knowledge over less than half a millennium. On the other hand, unbridled use of nature has led to a global crisis called climate change and is responsible for the suffering of innumerable other species—subject to man's experiments and displaced by man's encroachment. Finally, human beings have created the possibility of their own extinction, not only as a result of climate change, but also as a result of weapons of mass destruction they have fashioned. If used, nuclear arsenals around the world can annihilate the human species, along with the rest of the creatures on the planet.

A CRITICAL LOOK AT BACON'S ATTITUDE TOWARD NATURE

Ecofeminist and science historian Carolyn Merchant argues that during the Enlightenment—the period that followed the Scientific Revolution—nature became objectified. In *The Death of Nature*, she argues that nature was seen as a benevolent mother before the Scientific Revolution, and the prevailing attitude was one in which human beings cooperated with nature. They depended on nature and were interdependent with her. On the other hand, the authors of the Scientific Revolution sought to gain dominion over nature and force her to reveal her secrets. In one chapter in *The Death of Nature*, Merchant deconstructs Bacon's metaphors to show how he would have man force, torture, and enslave nature for his own purposes. Merchant quotes Bacon and says, "The new man of science must not think that the 'inquisition of nature is in any part interdicted or forbidden.' Nature must be 'bound into service' and made a 'slave,' put 'in constraint' and 'molded' by the mechanical arts. The 'searchers and spies of nature' are to discover her

The idyllic life in harmony with nature mostly has been relegated to the dustbin of history, and large population centers now exist in major metropolitan areas across the planet.

plots and secrets." Through the power of metaphor, Merchant argues, the archetypal magician—the forerunner of the scientist—is transformed from a servant of nature who

is grateful to receive her instruction to a slave master who would rule her.

Merchant also identifies Bacon as a spokesman for the capitalist state. She offers a critique of *The New Atlantis*, saying that the scientist is portrayed as a priest with "the power of absolving all human misery through science." She points out that the scientists of Bensalem decide which secrets will be shared and which will remain the property of Salomon's House. This is not unlike the current situation, in which scientists have appropriated certain types of knowledge with the use of technical language.

Highlighting the role of Salomon's House's in experimentation on animals and the creation of new species, Merchant argues that Bacon wanted to remove the ethical prohibitions against such work. This was in keeping with his program to reassert man's right to dominate nature, which Bacon—like many Christians—believed had been lost after man's fall and expulsion from paradise. Bacon's views support the

THE WONDERS OF SALOMON'S HOUSE OR FRANKENSTEIN'S MONSTERS?

The representative of Salomon's House who visits the shipwreck survivors in *The New Atlantis* describes the kinds of experiments that are performed on animals there:

> We have also parks and enclosure of all sorts of beasts and birds which we use not only for view or rareness, but likewise for dissections and trails; that thereby we may take light what may be wrought upon the body of man.
>
> By art likewise, we make them greater or taller than their kind is; and contrariwise dwarf them, and stay their growth: we make them more fruitful and bearing than their kind is; and contrariwise barren and not generative. Also we make them differ in colour, shape, activity, many ways. We may find means to make commixtures and copulations of different kinds; which have produced many new kinds, and them not barren, as the general opinion is. We make a number of kind of serpents,

> flies, fishes, of putrefaction; whereof some are advanced (in effect) to be perfect creatures, like be[a]sts or birds, and have sexes, and do propagate. Neither do we this by chance, but we know beforehand, of what matter and commixture what kind of those creatures will arise.

growth and progress of capitalism and the objectification of nature, Merchant says, as well as the practical application of science to human problems.

RELIGION AND SCIENCE

Merchant argues that the fathers of science in *The New Atlantis* have the trappings of a priestly sect and are revered, if not worshipped, by the inhabitants of Bensalem. And while Bacon does take pains to locate Bensalem's authority in the Christian tradition, reverence for science does seem to be the centerpiece of his utopian fragment. The idea that Bacon had the hidden agenda of displacing religion with science is refuted by historian Stephen McNight, who argues against the views of political philosophers like Howard White and Jerry Weinberger. White argues that the religious themes in *The New Atlantis* actually subvert Christian ideology and that Bacon justifies the pursuit of luxury in his utopian tale. Jerry Weinberger claims that Bacon merely uses religious language to veil his true secular agenda. Marina Leslie argues that Bacon supplants spiritual salvation with a material salvation, authored by human beings. McNight disagrees with these views. He believes Bacon had strong religious convictions that were the basis of his vision of political and material prosperity. He agrees that Bacon sought to take back man's dominion over nature lost after the Fall of Man, but that Bacon sees this quest as a restoration of the divine origins of natural philosophy. Whether Bacon had religious fervor is irrelevant to the import of his ideas. What cannot be denied is that science developed along a secular trajectory. Moreover, by the end of the seventeenth century, scientists had given themselves permission to probe nature's secrets without reservation and to move full speed ahead in their program to dominate the external world.

THE RESULTS OF NATURE'S SUBJUGATION

In 1700, the number of human beings on the earth was likely about 650 million, while the current population is about 7 billion and is projected to

Francis Bacon and others sought to reestablish man's ascendancy over nature, which was believed to have been lost in Adam and Eve's fall from grace and expulsion from Paradise.

reach 9.7 billion by 2050. While food shortages continue to be a problem, the Green Revolution, which took place from the 1930s to the 1960s, increased food production worldwide and put an end to pervasive famine. Today's famines are attributable to war and poverty, rather than the technical inability to produce enough food. Advances in medicine have been able to hold off pandemics, and life expectancy has risen dramatically in developed nations. Improvements in sanitation, health care, medicine, nutrition, and access to education also have contributed to the increase in human population.

On the other hand, increases in population are stressing natural resources, and massive water shortages are predicted over the next decades. Advances in agriculture have been partially achieved through genetic engineering. For example, genetically modified corn, wheat, and soy are changed in the laboratory to resist powerful pesticides. These industrial crops used to produce massive amounts of processed food are heavily sprayed, and as a result, weeds are becoming

Genetically engineered corn is an example of a GMO (genetically modified organism). It has a built-in *Bacillus thuringiensis* delta endotoxin that kills caterpillar larvae that can damage crops.

more resistant. A new breed of "super weeds" are getting more "super" by the year—thus requiring even more application of pesticide. Pesticides poison both crops and the environment. Pesticides sprayed on crops ensure that food is contaminated with glyphosate. Glyphosate is linked to increases in cancer and many other health problems. In a similar vein, the invention of antibiotics has wiped out many microbial-based diseases, but new variations are cropping up, as bacteria become more resistant to antibiotics.

The quality of life for people in developed countries has improved dramatically over the last three hundred years. Free public education through high school is available to all. University education is widely available as well, although it is becoming more expensive. For the most part, people in developed countries have indoor plumbing, electric lights, unlimited access to food, and heat and hot water. If they can't work, they get some (although not always adequate) help from the government, and debtors' prisons and slavery have been abolished. Human and civil rights have been expanded to previously disenfranchised groups—particularly women and minority groups in first-world democracies. People now have seemingly unlimited options in entertainment, and the technological revolution has created global connectivity and is changing the way we work, think, and live.

On the other hand, the gap between the haves and the have-nots is widening. Some people are predicting that, because of advances in technology, we will soon be facing a world in which there is not enough work for everybody. In the United States, some people say we have entered the era of the "carceral state," in which huge numbers of people—particularly minorities—are warehoused in increasingly privatized jails. While the advances of science and technology have given us more comfort and more time, leisure has bestowed upon us more anxiety and alienation. Family members often live at great distances from one another. Moreover, because of increased mobility, people are less likely to make lifelong friends. Lack of social support can make people feel unhappy and isolated. And, of course, the accelerating warming of the planet as a result of massive consumption of the fossil fuels that allow us to heat our homes, drive our cars, grow our food, run our computers, and so forth, has created a global crisis.

So how should we view Bacon and the Scientific Revolution? When we consider that the human species transitioned from hunter-gatherers to agriculturalists only some 12,000 years ago, we shouldn't be surprised that mistakes were made along that bumpy but accelerated road. The Scientific Revolution occurred only 400 years ago; as a result, human society has been changing at lightning speed. We were bound to make a lot of mistakes, some through hubris but most due to lack of foresight.

While Sir Francis Bacon is widely praised for his contributions to the Scientific Revolution, others criticize him for encouraging the objectification of nature.

Whether these mistakes will destroy us or take us beyond anything we can currently imagine is still an open question. We have every reason to be optimistic, however, since our species has been gifted with endless ingenuity.

TIMELINE

1561 Francis Bacon is born at York House, London, to Lady Anne Cooke Bacon and Sir Nicholas Bacon.

1564 Galileo Galilei is born in Pisa, Italy; William Shakespeare is born in Stratford-upon-Avon, England.

1573 Bacon enters Trinity College.

1579 Bacon returns from Paris after his father dies.

1582 Bacon gains admittance to the bar to practice law.

1584 Bacon first gains a seat in Parliament.

1592 Bacon declares "I have taken all of knowledge to be my province."

1596 Bacon named counsel extraordinary by the queen, Elizabeth I.

1597 Bacon publishes the first edition of his *Essayes*.

1601 Robert Devereux, Bacon's friend and patron, is arrested for treason; Bacon must help prepare the Crown's case.

1603 Elizabeth I dies; James I becomes the king of England.

1605 Bacon's *The Advancement of Learning*, which lays out a revised approach to learning and a plan for the reclassification of knowledge, is published.

1606 Bacon marries Alice Barnhem.

1613 Bacon becomes attorney general under James I.

1617 Bacon becomes a member of the House of Lords and lord keeper of the seal.

1618 Bacon becomes lord chancellor under James I.

1609 Bacon publishes *De Sapientia Veterum.*

1620 Bacon publishes *Novum Organum*, which advances his ideas about the "idols" that get in the way of dispassionate observation; he also revises Aristotle's approach to the scientific method.

1621 Bacon is accused of bribery, tried, and found guilty. He is stripped of public offices and turns all his attention to literary, philosophical, and scientific pursuits.

1624 Bacon publishes *The New Atlantis*, a visionary fragment about a society ruled by scientists.

1626 Bacon suffers from chills and weakness while doing a scientific experiment in the cold and dies shortly thereafter.

1660 The Royal Society of London is founded by Christopher Wren and other men of science. They are inspired by Bacon's Salomon's House, a fictional institute dedicated to "the study of the works and creatures of God."

GLOSSARY

ARISTOTELIANISM A philosophical attitude inspired by Aristotle's philosophy, especially one that relies on classical logic as expounded by Aristotle.

AXIOM A generally accepted or seemingly self-evident principle.

DEDUCTION A process of reasoning that begins with a hypothesis or generalization and then tests it through observation or experimentation. Deductive arguments move from the general or universal to the particular.

ECOFEMINISM A philosophy that argues that capitalistic society is paternalistic and male dominated and has split nature and culture by rejecting the nurturing, feminine side of life.

EMPIRICISM A philosophical theory that says that all knowledge is arrived at from data received through the senses.

EPISTEMOLOGY A theory of knowledge. Also a branch of philosophy that delves into how we know what we know and the limits of what we can know.

EUTHANASIA The practice of helping hasten a person's death when one's life becomes unbearable.

GENETIC ENGINEERING Changing an organism's characteristics by altering its genetic material.

HUMANISM A philosophy that began in the Renaissance

and which begins with the premise that people are basically good and can use reason to solve problems. Humanist philosophers focus on reason instead of religion.

HYPOTHESIS An explanation or educated guess about an observed phenomenon, which is then tested by additional observation and experimentation.

IDOL In Bacon's definition, notions deeply rooted in the mind that take hold of human understanding. In other contexts, an idol is an image representing a god.

INDUCTION A process of reasoning that formulates a hypothesis or generalization based on observation or experimentation. Inductive arguments move from the particular to the universal or general.

INQUISITION A Catholic court established to deal with people who violated the rules of the Church or spoke against its doctrines.

INSTAURATION A reinstitution, reestablishment, or reconstruction.

LOGIC A system for reasoning; a system of principles used to determine proof or validity.

METAPHYSICS In Bacon's usage, it refers to abstract thoughts or theories; more generally it is the branch of philosophy that deals with first principles—for example, being, time, and space.

PHENOMENON (plural PHENOMENA) An object of perception: a fact, an occurrence, an observation, or an experience.

PHYSICS In Bacon's usage, it refers to the study of matter; in current, conventional usage, it refers to the branch of science that studies matter and energy.

SCHOLASTICISM A medieval school of philosophy that applied Aristotle's logic to theological questions and eventually to other fields of study.

SECULAR Nonreligious; not tied to religion.

SYLLOGISM A logical argument in which a conclusion is drawn based on two assumed premises. Each premise shares a "term" (word or phrase) with the conclusion. The premises share a common term (called a middle term) that is not present in the conclusion. A syllogism may or may not be true.

TELOS A philosophical term that means the end purpose or goal, usually of a philosophical investigation.

For More Information

American Association for the Advancement of Science
PO Box 96178
Washington DC, 20090
(202) 326-6417
Website: http://www.aaas.org
This nonprofit organization promotes the advancement of science and fosters cooperation between scientists. It publishes the weekly science journal *Science* and has members in more than ninety countries.

American Philosophical Association
University of Delaware
31 Amstel Avenue
Newark, DE 19716
(302) 831-1112
Website: http://www.apaonline.org
This professional organization is open to high school and college students in North America. Membership dues are nominal. The organization supports scholarship in the field and career development.

Francis Bacon Society
Website: http://www.francisbaconsociety.co.uk

This literary association promotes the study of the Renaissance and has particular interest in Francis Bacon and William Shakespeare. Members continue to investigate the question of whether Bacon and Shakespeare were the same person.

The Royal Society
6-9 Carlton House Terrace
St. James's, London SW1Y 5AG
United Kingdom
+44 207 451 2500
Website: https://royalsociety.org
This highly regarded scientific society has counted dozens of history's most brilliant scientists as fellows. Its founders were inspired by the description of Salomon's House in *The New Atlantis.*

Society for Science & the Public
1719 N Street, NW
Washington, DC 20036
(202) 785-2255
Website: https://www.societyforscience.org
Founded in 1921, this group aims to promote the understanding and appreciation of science. It publishes *Science News*, and its website provides free

access to the journal's innumerable articles.

Society of Physics Students
1 Physics Ellipse
College Park, MD 20740
(301) 209-3007
Website: https://www.spsnational.org
This is a professional organization for students interested in science, specifically physics, although members include students in other scientific disciplines. The organization offers online publications, web resources, and opportunities to network.

WEBSITES

Because of the changing nature of internet links, Rosen Publishing has developed an online list of websites related to the subject of this book. This site is updated regularly. Please use this link to access the list:

http://www.rosenlinks.com/LOSR/bacon

For Further Reading

Augustyn, Adam. *Authors of the Medieval and Renaissance Eras: 1100 to 1660*. New York, NY: Britannica Educational Publishing, 2014.

Bauer, Susan Wise. *The History of the Renaissance World: From the Rediscovery of Aristotle to the Conquest of Constantinople*. New York, NY: W. W. Norton & Company, 2013.

Ellis, Robert P. *Francis Bacon: The Double-Edged Life of the Philosopher and Statesman*. Jefferson, NC: McFarland Company, 2015.

Guy, John. *Elizabeth: The Forgotten Years*. New York, NY: Viking, 2016.

Hannam, James. *The Genesis of Science: How the Christian Middle Ages Launched the Scientific Revolution*. Washington, DC: Regnery Publishing, 2011.

Principe, Lawrence. *Scientific Revolution: A Very Short Introduction*. Oxford, UK: Oxford University Press, 2011.

Roscoe, Kelly, and Mike Isle. *Aristotle: The Father of Logic*. New York, NY: Rosen Publishing, 2016.

Weston, Anthony. *A Rulebook for Arguments*. Indianapolis, IN: Hackett Publishing Company, 2009.

Withey, Michael, and Henry Zhang. *Mastering Logical Fallacies: The Definitive Guide to Flawless Rhetoric and Bulletproof Logic*. Berkeley, CA: Zephyros Press, 2016.

Bibliography

Bacon, Francis. *The Advancement of Learning*. Translated and edited by Joseph Devey. New York, NY: P. F. Collier and Son, 1901. http://oll.libertyfund.org/titles/1433.

Bacon, Francis. *The New Atlantis*. London, UK: 1627. http://www.gutenberg.org/files/2434/2434-h/2434-h.htm.

Bacon, Francis. *The New Organon or True Directions Concerning the Interpretation of Nature*. Translated by James Spedding, Robert Leslie Ellis, and Douglas Denon Heath in *The Works* (Vol. VIII). Boston, MA: Taggard and Thompson, 1863. http://www.constitution.org/bacon/nov_org.htm.

Cavendish, Richard. "The Execution of the Earl of Essex." *History Today* 51, no. 2 (February 2001). http://www.historytoday.com/richard-cavendish/execution-earl-essex.

Coates, Ta-Nehisi. "The Black Family in the Age of Mass Incarceration." *The Atlantic* (October 2015). http://www.theatlantic.com/magazine/archive/2015/10/the-black-family-in-the-age-of-mass-incarceration/403246.

Dickie, William M. "A Comparison of the Scientific Method and Achievement of Aristotle and Bacon." *The Philosophical Review* 31, no. 5 (Sept. 1922):

471–494.

Durant, William. *The Story of Philosophy.* New York, NY: Simon and Schuster, 1961.

The Economist. "The Royal Society: The Establishment of Science." January 7, 2010. http://www.economist.com/node/15214028.

Eiseley, Loren. *The Man Who Saw Through Time.* New York, NY: Charles Scribner's Sons, 1973.

Haidar, Zain. "UN Predicts Severe Water Shortages by 2030." The Weather Channel. March 23, 2015. https://weather.com/science/environment/news/water-shortage-united-nations-report.

Hamlyn, C. S. *A History of Western Philosophy.* New York, NY: Viking, 1987.

Kreis, Steven. "Lectures on Early Modern European History." The History Guide. 2002. http://www.historyguide.org/earlymod/earlymod.html.

Manchester, William. *A World Lit Only by Fire.* New York, NY: Little, Brown and Company, 1993.

McKnight, Stephen. "Francis Bacon's God." *The New Atlantis* (Fall 2005): 73–99.

Medievalists.net. "A Quick Guide to Medieval Monastic Orders." February 21, 2016. http://www.medievalists.net/2016/02/21/a-quick-guide-to-medieval-monastic-orders.

Merchant, Carolyn. *The Death of Nature: Women, Ecology, and the Scientific Revolution.* New York, NY: HarperCollins, 1990.

Paparella, Emanuel. "Medieval Monasticism as Preserver of Western Civilization." Metanexus. May 31, 2008. http://www.metanexus.net/essay/medieval-monasticism-preserver-western-civilization.

Petruzzelli, Michael. "Monasticism's Enduring Value." Catholic Culture.org. 2016. https://www.catholicculture.org/culture/library/view.cfm?recnum=7387.

Rossi, Paolo. *Francis Bacon: From Magic to Science.* Translated by Sacha Rabinovich. Chicago, IL: University of Chicago Press, 1968.

Rothchild, Irving. "Induction, Deduction, and the Scientific Method." The Society for the Study of Reproduction, 2006. http://www.ssr.org/sites/ssr.org/files/uploads/attachments/node/16/rothchild_scimethod.pdf.

Simpson, David. "Francis Bacon." Internet Encyclopedia of Philosophy. Retrieved November 4, 2016. http://www.iep.utm.edu/bacon.

Sorabella, Jean. "Monasticism in Western Medieval Europe." Heilbrunn Timeline of Art History. Retrieved November 4, 2016. http://www

.metmuseum.org/toah/hd/mona/hd_mona.htm.

Stokes, Philip. *Philosophy: 100 Essential Thinkers.* New York, NY: Enchanted Lion Books, 2003.

United Nations Department of Economic and Social Affairs. "World Population Projected to Reach 9.7 billion by 2050." July 29, 2015. http://www.un.org/en/development/desa/news/population/2015-report.htm.

Index

A

B

C

D

ABOUT THE AUTHOR

Maryellen Lo Bosco is a writer with a broad background in the humanities. She writes about literature, history, and philosophy and has taught English language arts in high school and expository writing in college. She also has many years of experience as an academic editor in the social sciences and has worked with writers on scholarly books in the field of psychoanalysis. Additional projects include writing literature guides and tutoring students in writing at Suffolk County Community College in Brentwood, New York.

PHOTO CREDITS

Cover, p. 1 (portrait) Stock Montage/Archive Photos/Getty Images; cover, p. 1 (background) Photos.com/Thinkstock; pp. 5, 14-15, 71 Private Collection/ Bridgeman Images; p. 13 Universal History Archive/Universal Images Group/ Getty Images; p. 17 Bob Thomas/Popperfoto/Getty Images; p. 19 Photo12/ Universal Images Group/Getty Images; pp. 23, 28-29, 74-75 Print Collector/ Hulton Archive/Getty Images; pp. 25, 61, 88-89 Heritage Images/Hulton Fine Art Collection/Getty Images; pp. 32-33 Prado, Madrid, Spain/Bridgeman Images; p. 36 Pictorial Press Ltd/Alamy Stock Photo; p. 39 Photo Researchers, Inc/Alamy Stock Photo; pp. 42, 84-85 DEA/A. Dagli Orti/De Agostini/Getty Images; p. 47 Culture Club/Hulton Archive/Getty Images; p. 49 DEA Picture Library/Getty Images; pp. 52-53 INTERFOTO/Alamy Stock Photo; p. 58 Heritage Images/ Hulton Archive/Getty Images; pp. 64-65 Pallava Bagla/Corbis Historical/Getty Images; pp. 66-67 Spencer Weiner/Los Angeles Times/Getty Images; p. 76 Leemage/Hulton Fine Art Collection/Getty Images; p. 80 Georgios Kollidas/ Shutterstock.com; pp. 90-91 Fedor Selivanov/Shutterstock.com; p. 94 View Pictures/Universal Images Group/Getty Images; back cover, pp. 8, 21, 34, 46, 57, 70, 82 agsandrew/Shutterstock.com; pp. 10, 11, 26, 27, 44, 54, 55, 68, 69, 78, 86, 87, 96-112 (background pattern) Ilya Bolotov/Shutterstock.com.

Designer: Brian Garvey; Editor: Amelie von Zumbusch; Photo Researcher: Bruce Donnola